thumb position studies

for the cello, book seven

by cassia harvey

CHP311

©2016 by C. Harvey Publications All Rights Reserved.

www.charveypublications.com

more information on the cover art can be found at www.gregharveygallery.com

Thumb Position Studies for the Cello
1

Book Seven: Stretching out of position

Cassia Harvey

©2016 C. Harvey Publications All Rights Reserved.

2

Hold thumb down, in the original position, for the entire line.
Keep first finger curved as it shifts.

Thumb Position Studies for the Cello, Book Seven

3

Hold thumb down, in the original position, for the entire line.
Keep first finger curved as it shifts.

simile

©2016 C. Harvey Publications All Rights Reserved.

4

Hold thumb down, in the original position, for the entire line.
Keep first finger curved as it shifts.

Thumb Position Studies for the Cello, Book Seven

5

Hold thumb down, in the original position, for the entire line.
Keep first finger curved as it shifts.

6

Hold thumb down, in the original position, for the entire line.
Keep first finger curved as it shifts.

7

Hold thumb down, in the original position, for the entire line.

8

Hold thumb down, in the original position, for the entire line.

Thumb Position Studies for the Cello, Book Seven

9

Hold thumb down, in the original position, for the entire line.
Keep second finger curved as it shifts.

10

Hold thumb down, in the original position, for the entire line.
Keep second finger curved as it shifts.

Thumb Position Studies for the Cello, Book Seven

11

Hold thumb down, in the original position, for the entire line.
Keep second finger curved as it shifts.

©2016 C. Harvey Publications All Rights Reserved.

12

Hold thumb down, in the original position, for the entire line.
Keep second finger curved as it shifts.

13

Hold thumb down, in the original position, for the entire line.

14

Hold thumb down, in the original position, for the entire line.

15

Hold thumb down, in the original position, for the entire line.

16

17

Hold thumb in the original position for each line.

18

Thumb Position Studies for the Cello, Book Seven

19

Creeping: Hold each finger down until the next finger is in place. Reach between notes, rather than jump.

©2016 C. Harvey Publications All Rights Reserved.

20

Creeping: Hold each finger down until the next finger is in place. Reach between notes, rather than jump.

21

Creeping: Hold each finger down until the next finger is in place. Reach between notes, rather than jump.

22

Creeping: Hold each finger down until the next finger is in place. Reach between notes, rather than jump.

23

24

* Hold 1st finger until you stretch back with the thumb.
Then lift 1st finger and play the thumb.

Thumb Position Studies for the Cello, Book Seven

25

* Hold 2nd finger and stretch back with the thumb.

©2016 C. Harvey Publications All Rights Reserved.

26

Thumb Position Studies for the Cello, Book Seven

27

Creeping: Hold each finger down until the next
finger is in place. Reach between notes, rather than jump.

28

Creeping: Hold each finger down until the next finger is in place. Reach between notes, rather than jump.

29

30

Creeping: Hold each finger down until the next finger is in place. Reach between notes, rather than jump. *Pick non-playing fingers up in the air as necessary.*

Thumb Position Studies for the Cello, Book Seven

31

Creeping: Hold each finger down until the next finger is in place. Reach between notes, rather than jump. *Pick non-playing fingers up in the air as necessary.*

©2016 C. Harvey Publications All Rights Reserved.

32

Creeping: Hold each finger down until the next finger is in place. Reach between notes, rather than jump. *Pick non-playing fingers up in the air as necessary.*

Thumb Position Studies for the Cello, Book Seven

33

Creeping: Hold each finger down until the next finger is in place. Reach between notes, rather than jump. *Pick non-playing fingers up in the air as necessary.*

©2016 C. Harvey Publications All Rights Reserved.

34

Creeping: Hold each finger down until the next finger is in place. Reach between notes, rather than jump. *Pick non-playing fingers up in the air as necessary.*

35

Creeping: Hold each finger down until the next finger is in place. Reach between notes, rather than jump.
Pick non-playing fingers up in the air as necessary.

36

Creeping: Hold each finger down until the next finger is in place. Reach between notes, rather than jump. *Pick non-playing fingers up in the air as necessary.*

Thumb Position Studies for the Cello, Book Seven

37

Creeping: Hold each finger down until the next finger is in place. Reach between notes, rather than jump. *Pick non-playing fingers up in the air as necessary.*

38

Creeping: Hold each finger down until the next finger is in place. Reach between notes, rather than jump.
Pick non-playing fingers up in the air as necessary.

Thumb Position Studies for the Cello, Book Seven

39

Creeping: Hold each finger down until the next finger is in place. Reach between notes, rather than jump.
Pick non-playing fingers up in the air as necessary.

©2016 C. Harvey Publications All Rights Reserved.

40

Creeping: Hold each finger down until the next finger is in place. Reach between notes, rather than jump. *Pick non-playing fingers up in the air as necessary.*

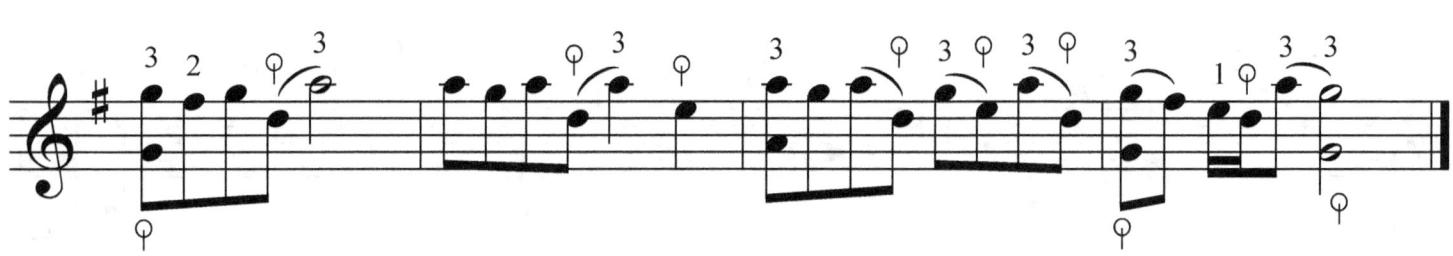

41

Creeping: Hold each finger down until the next finger is in place. Reach between notes, rather than jump. *Pick non-playing fingers up in the air as necessary.*

42

43

44

Creeping: Hold each finger down until the next finger is in place. Reach between notes, rather than jump. *Pick non-playing fingers up in the air as necessary.*

45

Creeping: Hold each finger down until the next finger is in place. Reach between notes, rather than jump.
Pick non-playing fingers up in the air as necessary.

Creeping: Hold each finger down until the next finger is in place. Reach between notes, rather than jump. *Pick non-playing fingers up in the air as necessary.*

46

www.ingramcontent.com/pod-product-compliance
Lightning Source LLC
Chambersburg PA
CBHW051426070526
44584CB00023B/3593